SOMETIMES A WOMAN

By the same author:

Finally, the Moon (2017)

SOMETIMES A WOMAN

KIMBERLY K. WILLIAMS

RECENT
WORK
PRESS

Sometimes a woman
Recent Work Press
Canberra, Australia

Copyright © Kimberly K. Williams, 2021

ISBN: 9780645009064 (paperback)

A catalogue record for this
book is available from the
National Library of Australia

Cover image: Allyson Williams-Yee ©2021, reproduced with permission
Cover design: Recent Work Press
Set by Recent Work Press

recentworkpress.com

PL

For my mama, Elaine K. Williams,
who was there at the beginning

Contents

Preface

A couple of months after I moved to Phoenix, Arizona, in 2012, I travelled south to Tombstone for a weekend. There I found myself in a curious space. The town made famous by the gunfight at the OK Corral had been refashioned for tourism. Wooden planks lined the streets that hosted a variety of businesses, including saloons, restaurants, souvenir stands, and sweet shops. On the east end of the town stood one of the few authentic structures from the era that Wyatt Earp and his brothers made legendary, the Cage Bird Theatre, which, though dusty and cluttered, was mostly intact and functioned as sort of a unorganised and casual museum. Walking through, visitors saw Faro tables, doorways that led to spaces that were once the cribs of the working girls, and antique items, like books and photos, which memorialised the era. They also might have noticed the bullet holes that remained in a few of the wall-hangings in the room closest to the street.

Among the dust and bric-a-brac on one wall, I noticed a revealing photo of Josie Marcus, Wyatt Earp's third wife, who is thought to have been a prostitute herself prior to their relationship. Also on display were permits filed by the women to work legally as prostitutes, giving dates and the amount of fees paid. Something about the details of the permits ignited my imagination, and I began to wonder about the lives of these prostitutes. Who were they? What did their voices sound like? What were their daily lives like?

When these women are depicted in movies or books and even in folk songs like "The Yellow Rose of Texas," they tend to be depicted flatly and predictably: the fallen woman, the prostitute with the heart of gold, the luring vixen, and so on. I started reading history books and taking notes, learning about the lives of these women. Over the next few years, I visited some of the towns and places where they lived, ranging from Jerome, Arizona, to Cripple Creek, Colorado. My notes would lead to journal entries, and the entries developed into poems, which eventually led to this book.

What I learnt through my research was how essential these women were to the economic and social fabric of the West—that wide imaginative space that exists on so many levels. They helped establish the communities that now comprise the Rocky Mountains and southwest territories of the United States—what is commonly referred to as the 'Wild West'. What I also realised is that these women had complex lives, hard to pin down with words, which made the endeavour that much more fulfilling to pursue. In addition, I purposefully left out both women and settings from California as my research revealed it to be a much more complex situation with so many of the 'working girls' being slaves brought over from China, what we now would likely call human trafficking. I did not feel that having only a handful of poems from that part of the West could acknowledge that complexity.

In my research, I didn't encounter a single woman who used her own legal surname. Names were regularly changed to protect the identity of the families the women came from, even when they were leaving harsh familial circumstances. Some of the women used a few different aliases, which created practical challenges as I tracked down biographical information. In the women's own era, the aliases created difficulties when it came to identifying bodies, notifying families of the deceased, keeping census records, and so on. In this book, where the titles are the names of women, I used the names they were known by in their work, not their birth names.

As I edited the poems, what I encountered often surprised me, though I had written it myself. Sometimes, when drafting these poems, the voices of the women would come through as clearly as a tune that I might hear in my head. However, the best part of this project was the unexpected comprehension and richness that the research and subsequent writing process allowed. It offered me an entirely new understanding of and appreciation for women's roles, lives, and legacies in the nineteenth century American West.

I Am Legend: Emily West Morgan

They made a song out of me.
You heard it? *The Yellow Rose
of Texas*. Sometimes they still
sing it, and it makes me laugh.

No one knows anything, yet
someone put a chapter in a book
about me, anyway, Emily West.
Go West, Emily. I was born

free in Connecticut. Mostly
it's circumstance—moving to Texas
and not fleeing before it was too
late when that general, named like

he was some great saint—Santa Anna—
a woman saint, no less, had come along.
Mostly, like Etta Place, my job was
to disappear. My job was not to open

my legs to that Mexican. I didn't service
that gringo Morgan, either. I only kept his
house. But men will remember women
how they will, and someone had to write

that damn song, and that song had to persist
in its awful down-through-the decades ear-
worm way, and when I realized
that, well, I didn't stick around

to tell. I was not a whore. I was not
of Texas. I was born free
when we were mostly not, and if
the true version of my time in

Texas messes up the lyrics just a little,
then so be it. So it is. I know nothing
about those stupid roses and I
only know about my time in town,

and I don't know that general. But I do
know about being yellow and about being
mostly free, but nobody ever asks about that.

What's In

a name? Darkened
angel, fallen
flower, woman
of the half
world, red
light lady,

sporting
girl, soiled
dove, frail
sister—all
doing what
she had
to do.

Three Doves at the Edge of Prescott

Far off, it looked like a tiny chicken—one
of those skinny white ones you think to stuff
a pillow with—pecking at the ground like a telegraph
operator tapping. Mollie and I walked.

We laughed when we came upon it
and it didn't startle. 'That is one fat rock
pigeon,' she said. I said, 'Looks like a dove.'
She said, 'Same difference.' That
blonde has a smart crown. We stood

still. 'It's so very white.'
She nodded, 'Not all doves are soiled.'
I asked, 'Do you think it's a sign?' She linked
her arm in mine, and together we walked home.

Lil Powers, Salida, Colorado

I was a schoolhouse teacher,
but the salary was low and the children
sweet but tedious. A man can be
tedious, too, but you only need to pay

attention one at a time. I could do more
and get farther providing pleasure
than instructing in letters and arithmetic.
When I elected to run cribs rather than live

in a parlor house, I surprised the town.
I learned to be in charge and don't
let no one own me. Soldiers that come
through here insist they fight for freedom

even as the army don't allow them
to desert. I say liberty lies down
the unexpected trail.

Lydia Taylor, Kansas and Wyoming

I remember the first time
I realized clouds could move.
I was lying on the grass, facing
the sky, and saw a rabbit chasing
the dog and laughed, for everyone
knows it's supposed to be the other
way around. But clouds see it different.

I went home to tell Mama
what I saw, but she was tending
the young ones and trying to hang
wash with the baby on her hip.
'Mama!' I yelled, and she yelled
not to holler. 'But the clouds are
moving,' I said. She said, 'They do.'

I don't think she realized that the world
was about to break apart, what with the
pile of wash and the baby's screams.
Good God, my mama could just cuss
to incite a storm, but I just had to make
my point, so I said again, 'Those clouds—
there—they move!' and I pointed at the sky.

She sighed and said, 'Sarah, clouds
is supposed to move.' And I asked,
'Even those giant cotton ones?'
They looked like they flew right
off the spindle and grew fat picking
off the cottonwoods they floated over
in the night. Mama had a wooden clothespin
tucked in her mouth, so she only nodded.

I looked up at the blue space above
the patch of Kansas that day and watched
my little sisters chase my dog Sandy
beneath the stretch of line and
flapping sheets, and I wished hard,
feeling my heart puff like it was full
of rain, that the clouds would quit
their march, so it didn't all have to end
and Papa wouldn't return home
swinging his anger like an ax,
chasing me down the cellar steps
until I tumbled in the turnips.

Sometimes when a man's on top
and he's taking too long and I
don't have much to do I summon
those Kansas clouds and tempt
them to drift across Wyoming, hoping
they arrive with cottonwood tufts followed by
hard rain to wash away my sins.

Calamity Explains Gut Rot

You heard of me. I
know it. What's my plain
name? Say it. I wasn't a crack

shot. I was a crackpot, a drunk and bad
at drinking. I couldn't negotiate
my booze. Because

I could aim a rifle and because
I have a snatch, I am the stuff
of legends, legends that leave

out the gambling and the whoring
and the swollen splitting head-
aches. It's a big word, *unrequited*,

but I manage when I'm sober.
I paid my way with my coochie
and had a mouth to slay

a sailor. Stuff that
into your legend and suck it.

Queen of Ketchikan, Dolly Arthur

Now, come on. Admit it: that's
just fun to say: Queen of Ketchikan.
I mean, who's to say that Ketchikan
would even have a queen, and who
would want to reign over such a God-
forsaken place? I worked half

a century, choosing my trade. No
one forced me. My little place just
off the boardwalk with my fancy sign-
in book for clientele. I charged one hundred
percent more than any other gal. And that,
dear reader, is how I earned my crown.

Soiled Dove, Tombstone, AZ

That dove lay still as a nickel
at the bottom of a purse. The cat's
mouth clamped its body in a letter C. What
to do now? The cat is preparing
breakfast. The dove has made
its peace. *St. Francis, St. Anthony, and any*
saint who assists animals, please

intercede. I hollered, jumped up
and down in my bloomers, my hair tangling
in the hot wind. And that cross-
eyed black-and-white cat opened her mouth,
as if to holler back. And that bird, faster
than an angel with its wings lit afire, left three
floating feathers and vanished toward the sky.

For Millie Who Never Rested, On the Seventh Day

The rain
finally carried
Millie away after
she stained the street
for many days—six if
you're counting—her blood
smeared into a crescent where she
was run down and her body first lay right
across from the brothel, before I wrapped her
torn tenderness in a blanket and howled and begged
and someone carted her away. Daily, I stared at the dried
remains after the sun came up. In a place that never rains, where
heat just drains the green out of the cholla or even a saguaro, sears
purple from the prickly pear, the rain—like God or someone ordered up
a fat cloud full of water—came heaving down and rammed a river through the road,
and Millie's faded redness lifted, and her little chunks of flesh, too, washing her away.

Belle Grant, Denver, CO

I kept waiting for him to appear like a ghost,
like a sunrise, like a silhouette on the horizon
expands into shape and becomes clarity

before your eyes. Like a coin in the street
appears after the first days of May when the mud
finally dries. All these ways I just

kept vigil—by the window or tucked
under a blanket, trying to quit the smell
of the one who'd departed. I'd brush my hair

and imagine who could wear boots big
enough to carry me away. Who could make
me honest and clean? I worked and waited

and wondered while putting money on the side,
and asked Lil to come with me to Salt Lake. Maybe
we'd make more money there. Maybe meet a nice

Mormon man. We stopped off in Pueblo.
That night, mama came and sat on my bed and said,
'Belle, you carry on this way, we ain't never

gonna meet in heaven. You will be lost to me truly. And
I crave to see my daughter again.' Lil went on to Utah.
I returned to Denver with mama's ghost in tow. I counted

my coins, pulled out my sewing and found steady
work at the Salvation Army. All that time waiting
and wondering and whoring and waiting, No boots.

No strong arms to carry
me off like a prize. Just Mama coming
in a dream and rousing me from the nightmare.

Old Deadwood Days

A found poem taken from the words of author Estelline Bennett from her book.

Wealth dug out of the mines created no class
distinctions. In everything else
the contrasts were sharp and clear. Days divided in
high noons and sudden nights. There were no golden

pink dawns and no purple twilights. Winter
mornings were dark until the high sun leaped
from behind White Rocks. Sometimes it found clouds
floating around way below. The seasons came in

with a bang and there you were. Only autumn slipped
in gently at the end of a summer—bright days and crisp, cool
nights and an occasional flurry of snow, trailing its purple
veils over the gorgeousness of scarlet sumac, golden

aspen and scrub oak. The lovely night ladies—pretty,
beautifully gowned, and demure mannered—were
known by face and name to everybody.
But their little span of glory was too brief to leave

any illusion in our minds about the desirability
of such lives. They collected their wages of
sin under our very eyes. We saw
them on the street, in the stores, at the theater on the rare

occasions of a play at Nye's Opera House or Keimer Hall.
And then, two or three years later, we saw these same
girls pallid and shabby slipping furtively down
the alley that ran back of Main street, in quest of the price

of a drink or a shot of dope. In pathetically little while,
they disappeared. Once in a long time one of them married
and escaped this fate. Some of them avoided it by
the route of poison or the little gun. Without anyone

calling our attention to it, we accepted the inevitable end.

Whoring Explained Five Ways, Plus One Wonderment

1. At some point, every whore leaves
her mama unless her mama
just deserts her first.

2. No whore goes home for Christmas.

3. Sometimes he donates his name
and the clap to you before he splits.

4. Many whores (like me)
are married. Legally married
don't mean going home to him,
don't mean he loves you. Don't
even mean he ignores you,
though if you're lucky he will,
but mostly he'll want you to chip
in to subsidize the gambling.

5. Silence ain't
compliance. It's just
silence. (I hear
women are marching back
east with sashes and signs.)

6. There's a new word
I hear, *suffragette,*
and I wonder what it means.

Fancy Rita, Jerome, AZ

You think you've had a bad day? You
haven't had a bad day until you've
had a bad day and then
you have to go down

on a miner and blow
him for two bits. Ain't never
fun servicing a man with your mouth. You can pretend
otherwise, and there's lots of reasons

you might have to, given that most
women are wives or whores. But the truth is that
it just sucks when it's shoved in
there, his shaft rubs your teeth

and he wants you to clean
his rod with your tongue. It's worse
when they're chubby. My mouth ain't that
wide, and miners don't wash too

often and, by God, when they actually do
bother to soap their hands and face, they sure
don't do anything about the stench down
there. You want the real definition of

soiled? Look inside a miner's pants.
You'll only do it once. If you smile
when you do it and act a little friendly,
he might toss a copper your way and give

you a thick and juicy whisky kiss.
Then at the end of the day, after I do half
a dozen muddy miners, I pay a share to Miss
Banters and watch her grow fat off my mouth.

She's been running girls so long, I figure the last
time she had to suck a man's prick I was about six.
Whores grow up fast. And we learn quick how
one bad day ain't so

different than one
good day, least not in this line of work.

Apple on a String:
Velma Lober, Murray, Idaho

Nine months out of the year
my counterparts arrived by dog
sled. I arrived by carriage in July.
But it's more of a story if you slide
into town in the back of the pack.

I was a dancing girl, a sporting
girl. Truly, I didn't mind
so much, but you
just get so tired of the miners. You
just do. They have no more luck

digging through a woman than
they have panning for gold. I
thought to try it myself—the
panning part—and found
it's back-breaking work,

even trying for that placer gold
that looks like it's floating near
the top, like you could just scoop
your hand through the icy cold
and just lift it, flirting with the sun,

right out of the water. I went
back to miners after so many
days of soaked stockings
and freezing toes, and, good God,
my back angry and hollering from all

the bending, I'd just rather be lying
on it, I guess, until I took a shining
to a miner and he took a shining to me.

Then, I no longer did 'housework'.
He showed me how to lift that

gold from beneath the rushing water.
We had a cabin, and I cooked, and we
even had a little fun. But damned if
he didn't contract that pneumonia
and was dead within three days.

It ain't easy going back to housework
when you've been taking it
easy. But I was only his common
law wife, common as a housefly
in July, and his parents showed

up and took the claim and the cabin.
If you think I'm giving you a sad
story, you'd be wrong. I ain't.
I didn't have much luck with gold,
but I struck love twice, and this time

we were married legal. And to show
we were consummated and everything,
I invited the town to the saloon to celebrate
my lucky strike. And the bartender
tied an apple to a string and dropped

it from the ceiling into a bucket
of water and set it on the bar,
and my new man and I snuck
upstairs so we could demonstrate
our happiness to each other, and

throughout our demonstration in the room
above the bar, that apple jumped
and wiggled and bobbed so there
would be no doubt—none. That I was
proper his, and what was his was mine.

Jennie Banters, Jerome, AZ

We all end
up dead. Some
of us shot four

times, the final
shot close
range with the barrel

locking me against
the ground,
indicating where

I was headed. Four
bullets piercing four
times, just to be

sure I died. I did. Mostly
no one knows who
we were, no one

knows if we whistled
while bathing or laughed
pinning clothes to the line.

No one thinks about
us, except for Etta Place and Big
Nose Kate, Mattie and Josie—

anyone associated with
an Earp. No one knows
us. Remembering

us is like locating
an unmarked
coffin already

in the ground. Once
I used my hands
to dig up

a box. Inside
slept my boy. By
then, I ran

the house for
the women who
serviced them. Those

soiled doves—dirty
like the earth that encases
caskets—each one

was fertile, too.

Bride of the Multitude

I imagine the letter
deposited at the dock, gliding
over the broad

Atlantic waves, landing
in New York, being sorted
then bagged, finding

the train, crossing the plains
to Denver to ride the ruts
that take the stagecoach

up another two thousand
feet—unless by sled
if it snows. Yet

it never arrives where
I sit on the porch inhaling
pine mist after rain.

Sometimes a Woman:
Hattie LaPierre, Wyoming

Well, I shot him
dead, but only after
he shot off my big

toe. I fired the bullets into his chin
and his back, and it took him four
damn days to die. But he

died and my work was finally done.
You gonna make me a whore,
you gonna make all those men

stick it in me, you gonna find out
what I have inside. All those men
paying me and me acting like it's

normal every time they sprayed
their venom into me. *Sometimes*
a woman has had enough. A handful

of months in the pen was worth
escaping that living hell. I was pretty
once and in love with Harry

Black whose heart bears the color
of his name. When he smacked
his hand against my jaw, I knew

his own chin had it coming. *Do*
you know how to walk
toeless in pointed boots?

Do you know how it jars
to have men knock you
around from the inside

out? I asked him these
questions and he never did
answer. So I silenced him
for good.

Maxine, Tombstone, Arizona

'Elderly men would do well
to ask for Maxine. She is especially
adept at coping with matters peculiar to advanced
age and a general rundown condition,' reads my card.

It's true that I work with the further along in life. Sometimes
when a man has marched so many miles toward the end
of his battle, his sword gets a little dull. My specialty
is to sharpen it. Think about it:

by then a man has usually saved a little money
and he's also not looking so far into the distance,
so he's willing to spend a little, too. Those that need
their swords whetted and shined just a little? They tend

to be good tippers. Over here, on the shady side
of the street, I've used their swords to carve my niche.

Annie Groves, Wyoming

His name was the kind
kids giggle at every single time:
James C. Passwater. I wish
he only passed me water

instead of the clap. When
I was only nineteen,
my kisser ballooned
and peeled like a rotting

peach. Then it looked to the end
of my days, every damn one, like a strip
of rancid bacon pinned to my lower
lip. Nobody wants you then. No-

body will pay for your body.
How did I stand
that sentence in prison? Gladly
knowing that I sent him galloping

out of Wyoming. And really,
the governor went soft as a ripe
melon once he saw that slice of
pig above my chin. He might just

be a little partial to pork. True, it might've
been a longer stay if Mr. Passwater had died.
But he didn't die. Four bullets lodged
beneath his skin, and still that bastard lived.

Sadie Orchard, Kingston, NM

'It had always been her dream to become a respected Victorian woman, and prostitution made that difficult.'
—*Michael Rutter,* Boudoirs to Brothels: The Intimate World of Wild West Women

Ten mouths is a lot to feed, and most of us missed meals. I left home at fifteen and went west. What other way was there to go?

Miners rushed to the Black Range Mountains to play with silver. So I went that way, too. Sometimes a man feels lonely, and you can work some money out of him keeping him company.

My dream was to go to England. Despite my hungry childhood, I could read and write and run my business and buy myself petticoats and hats with feathers. I read everything about that kingdom,

and once Ying started cooking for me, I'd ask him to bake scones, which he made proper enough to drink with tea.

I ran a clean business. My girls dressed respectfully. Your grandmothers would not have taken exception.

I would close my eyes and imagine walking cobblestone streets in my leather boots, my bustle coming up behind me, small green umbrella in my gloved hand, marking the stones as I walked.

Geraniums waved from windows in the row houses. But when I opened my eyes, I was in Kingston instead of Kensington. The best I could do was look refined.

Only that man, that man who vexed me into marrying him and crossed me so many times after that? I tried to shoot him—several times. He didn't leave

me a choice. That man had a dandy handlebar mustache and a fashion to flirt. I have since found that a man with a fancy mustache will often fancy himself.

That man had nothing to hang his hat on besides his mustache and a rich mama, but rich mamas don't come for free.

For a while, being his wife made me respectable. What else can I say? The hotel and restaurant were mine. Once we were up and running, we didn't need his mama's money. I didn't even need

the brothel. But he could not break his mama's force, and I could never mind respectability when I was mad enough to load and lock.

Every time I aimed at that dandy of a man, the bullet parted air. Except one time I nicked the toe of his boot. I should have practiced more.

In the end, I wouldn't have hit a cow if she stood in front of me mooing, and I was forced to divorce.

Laura Evens, Leadville and Salida, Colorado

Here's the secret: you can start off at sea-level in Alabama and end
up living at 10,000 feet before life's done, and though the journey
starts off slow and hot and wet as a swamp, you can wonder
how you ended up here almost frozen

along the way. I expect the religious call it fate or destiny or God's
will until they're in my parlor wanting a new roof for their house
of God, and I donate the money so that the unholy and the holy

remain covered equally. But it ain't God's will, don't
you know. It's mine.

Miss Dora B. Topham,
Ogden and Salt Lake City, Utah

They say I looked like a schoolmarm, and I expect I did. When I dressed, I buttoned myself all the way up like a closed theatrical curtain. How else is one to successfully run a brothel in a Mormon state? One must look the part. I perched my glasses across my nose, and I gave every one of my girls the teacher glare when they squabbled or got out of line. Drama only invites the authorities. That's what I always told them. There'd be times that the city council would get a bee in its bonnet, and deputies and the sheriff would respond by sweeping the trash off the streets. That's when you want to look proper, so they look past you and fix their gazes down the road. I turned certain girls away, too. I only wanted the ones who didn't mind. I didn't want girls too young – they had to be sixteen or older, and they had to make a case for staying. Orphaned. Widowed. Abandoned. I'd give them a chance and pay their doctor's bills. But I wouldn't deal with runaways. My ladies knew upfront my take, and I never took a penny more. I also never gave out loans, so they never owed and could leave when they wanted. I built a brothel with one hundred cribs and hand-selected girls and called it the Stockade. The building swallowed an entire city block. City hall wanted to corral the local ladies in one arena for the purposes of regulation and control, and I was just following the flow of opportunity. 1908 we broke ground. We made it four years. But they still couldn't keep the city streets clean, and the venture failed. I hope they were surprised that there were more than one hundred working women so close to Brigham Young's remains. They razed that behemoth building and left that big block vacant, like one hundred whores and one schoolmarm madam never spent forty-eight months defining the desires of all those men.

Madam Mattie Silks Explains from Beyond, Denver, Colorado

Navigating Prohibition and then the Depression was like riding long distance on a horse without a saddle.

We sold the House of Mirrors to the Buddhists
and they opened up a Temple. Later, they sold it
to the chefs, and now you have fine dining. Laura
Bell's brothel is now a nursing home. Along Colorado
Avenue in Old Colorado City, a SnoWhite Laundry
sits in the spot where Jesse James's brother, Frank,
dealt Faro. It was a time. You might have enjoyed

a moment within if you were a man with some means.
I knew what those men liked. In the meantime, I do not
recommend romanticizing the unfamiliar. If you didn't live
then, you best leave it out of your imagination. Nothing
but the mirrors and the dresses were pretty. Everything
else gets soiled by human hands. You can shut up

a brothel. You can sell it to the holy. But you can't close
up a man's pants when he wants to leave them open.

On the Art of Whoring:
Laura Evens, Colorado

You don't get to be an artist
        when you're a whore. Who decides
these things? Some say a whore lacks vision,
        is capable of only one trade. Who knows
what I see? Art, like whoring, must surmount
        fear. When accomplished well, art
and whoring require the subtle and intimate
        manipulation of the buyer. If anyone
writes a book about art, I won't be in it. If anyone
        writes a book about whoring, you'll
find me sprinkling wonder like soil over a coffin
        by page one.

Kitty Explains Guthrie, Salida, CO

Who gives a whore money
to take her orders?
Guthrie is who. That
man, afraid to cross

his wife, is obedient as a dog.
He puts his coin in the box,
and I say, 'Guthrie, take off
your boots'. And he complies.

I say, 'Guthrie, clean your
cock,' and I'll be damned
if he doesn't pull out his
hanky and dip it in the wash

basin every time. He flies
into my crib in a fury
banging around in his big
black boots, fuming at his missus,

and in one request he goes all
soft even as he gets hard. He
sports a mustache furry enough
to run up a tree. Sometimes

I wonder if I ordered
him to shave that damned
rodent off his face, would he?
You cannot trust a man

who spends his time primping
in a looking glass or cleaning
his rifle but who has no time to straighten
out his problems. But I get paid

not to trust. That Guthrie wants
to kiss me down there and give me
pleasure, like he isn't my fifth john
of the night. I tell him, 'Guthrie, no

fanfare'. And he obeys and obliges.
Between his wife, his vanity, and the sheer
strain of his own pliability (which

incites his own anger), it won't be long
before his cock stops
cold like a broken clock.

Jessie, Leadville, CO

I ended up here at ten thousand
feet where you have to touch
fire to bite away the cold.

The colder the weather, the more
men will pay for warmth. Ducky don't
even drop his trousers and I can barely

gather up my skirts before he's fixing
to raise his body temperature
a spate. The cold

up here is like a man: it always
has its hands on you, but never where
you want to be touched.

Some Nights

            you are afraid
of everything: the bullets tucked
in each chamber, the pistols snug
inside their holsters, sleeping leather
against steel. Violence, like a baby,
awakens with a start. You are afraid

of the boots, filthy and hard as the men
who fill them, mean as the whisky
that tanks them. You are afraid
of the horses that trot down the street,
their tails swishing like whips, their
snorts and whinnies reminders that
you have no leverage, nothing to push

against with your legs raised in the night.
You are afraid of your hands, which take
the tokens, and your palms that turn
their fumy mouths away. You fear next
week, next month, next year, when gravity
and time invite your tricks elsewhere. You are
afraid of the room with the flickering light, but
you are also afraid of the flame. Most of all,

you fear the cold, which squeezes the breath
right out of your throat, like the boulder
that flattens the soil, like a pastor's glance
that sets you back. Everything you touch
hardens as anxiety tumbles
in your stomach like
a stone, presses up, shoves your heart between
your ribs, splintering the bone.

May Day Asserts, Boulder, CO

                    She pushed and I pulled
          her close enough
that she pinched
                    and I punched and we
          tumbled over
together, and she hollered
                    and kicked and I
          spat and screamed and she
scratched and I bit
                    and when the sheriff came
          along, I told him what
happened and cried out
                    some fat tears and showed him
          the red marks streaking my neck,
and he fined me $20.00 despite.

Susan Brown Responds, Boulder, CO

It is said that I have a 'permanent seamy' reputation. Well,
'Puta' dwells inside 'reputation'—I've been called that enough
by men who speak different languages. Just seems that 'puta' is an easy

word to spit. And it's true. I enjoy a good fracas. Or, better, a burning
brothel, so long as it ain't mine. I am partial to a good roasting.
'Love your enemy,' says that book, but I ain't good. We

already established that. Madam May Day is only getting
what she has coming. We go tit
for tat. She's incinerated my bordello,

several times, and I've returned the favor in kind.
When we finally came to blows that day in July, no one
was surprised. I built the Bon Ton, the second finest building

in Boulder and filled it with reliable whores. I build for strong.
You want to tussle with me? I ain't afraid. I ain't afraid of anyone.
I ain't afraid of the law. I ain't afraid of revenge. And I ain't afraid of fire.

Janey in Her Crib,
Somewhere Out West

From the upstairs
window I could
see the western

bluebird flitting
in the cottonwood's
branches, and even

though nightly I am in
the arms of men,
it's not

safe, not
the way that bird
felt himself part of that

tree at home hopping
along the bark, not
even wondering if he

belonged, just knowing
and nesting among
the branches—like me,

making his home right
where he slept. The light
was so bright

out the window, brilliant
yellow dancing off
the leaves with a band

of clouds advancing
from the west, a great grey
shield rising in the distance.

What the Quiet Whore Observes

His control is a weight
she has learned to bear.
She would be too light

without it. She might float
away—like one of those
giant balloons hovering

over the outskirts of a fair,
the kind with a heavy, hanging
basket. She might be free. Above

all, nothing scares her more
than a thought of open
sky, so she keeps her

head down and her
hands busy. She has learned to play
the piano. This he permits since

she's in the saloon and it
makes the customers happy. He likes
a snappy tune with his whisky. He yanks

her hair and pinches purple into her arms.
She used to defy him by day-
dreaming. But now she cannot

see her destination with so much
haze masking the view: a wooden
stake on the cemetery's edge,

a rock set at the top of the rectangle
of soil, the weight bearing down,
pressing a parcel of regret.

Silence Is Golden:
Josie Parker, Prescott, AZ, 1878

After a while, I learn to ignore
the noises—Mary, named after the Blessed
Mother herself, crying out in the next crib
so late on Saturday that it's really

Sunday arrived. Shots from the street,
usually preceded by drunk hollering, multiply
during the full moon. The noise magnifies
the weekend after Payroll Friday at the mines.

Of course, business is booming then, and
I'm too busy myself to listen and poke
into other people's lives. The hard
part is when it's slow, and the girls squabble,

and Johnny, out of boredom, picks a fight
with Sadie, who only obliges by calling
him a cocksucker. I will improve
my station. One day

I won't be stuck in the middle
crib with the walls that amplify every
cough, fart and sneeze. I'll have lace
curtains covering a true glass pane,

and I'll join Miss Sadie on the porch
with the jasmine, our only quiet neighbor,
early in the evening before the men
blow in like the smell of hundreds of cattle

being herded right through town. Jasmine shows
how silence can twist so lovely on the vine. Mean-
time, Jenny ha!s with her fake laughter in bursts
like bullets, and Old Dan bangs the keys

of the piano. Mr. Beatty smacks Mollie.
Her skin sounds out but she's learned
not to yell. When the john is quiet
and says no more than the final grunt,

I just lie here, craving
silence. Listening is one kind
of prayer. These evenings, the jasmine
and I beseech the Almighty

in tandem while I remind myself
that ignoring is surviving—and hoping is, too.

Roll Call of the Fancy Ladies of Yavapai County

(found in Jan McKell's Wild Women of Prescott, *AZ)*

Part I—Mistresses of Yavapai County, 1864

Pancha Acuna, born in México, Mariana
Complida, México, Teodora Días, México,
Nocolasa Frank, México, Andrea Galinda,
married, born in New Mexico, Rosa García,
México, Perfecta Gústalo, Tucson, Santa
López, mistress of Negro Brown, age 17,
México, Isabella Madina, México, María no
last name, México, Laguda Martínez, Tucson,
Francisca Méndez, no city given, Arizona,
Juana Miranoa, México, Donanciana Pérez,
México, Catherine Revere, age 40, México,
Ascensión Rodríguez, born in México, 35,
Sacramenta, no last name, age 20, México.

Part II—Mistresses of Yavapai County, 1870 Census

Nellie Stackhouse, born in Pennsylvania,
Mollie Sheppard, born in Ireland, Maggie
Taylor, age 19, born in California, Ginnie
McKinnie, age 18, born in New York. Mary
Anschutz, a.k.a. Jenny Schultz, no birthplace
listed, age 18, will be murdered in two months.

Part III—Mistresses of Yavapai County, 1880 Census

Nellie Rogers, born in Illinois, lived next door
to Mollie Sheppard. Elysia Garcia, age forty, lived
with six unnamed 'Mexican girls' who ranged in age
from sixteen to twenty-eight. Maria Quavaris, Pancha
Bolona, and Joan Arris, all from Sonora, ages seventeen
to twenty-eight, dwelled together. Living with them,
Savana Deas, born in Arizona, eight months old.

Broncho Liz Tells It Frankly

We were supposed to be flying straight, doing things
right. He got the divorce. I retired. We got married.

Then, while we were in Murray, he slept with that
actress, Frankie Howard. You should've met her—

dumb as a donkey. Did she shoot Charlie? I don't
know. I didn't take the time to ask. All I know is

he come back leaking blood from his thigh with a tear
in his trousers the size of your thumb. Charlie wanted it

repaired—his leg, his pants—all of it. But I thought, *if
you want to get shot, I'll get you*

shot. So I said to him sweet as smoke from fine tobacco,
'Charlie, come get fixed.' But he knew better. By the time

he arrived on my side of the room, he had his fist to my face.
But, honey, I don't miss. You want to fly

crooked when we're supposed to fly
straight? Why, I'll assist. The Derringer and I added three

holes to Charlie's collection. He died and because he smacked
me first, I walked free.

What Sadie Saw

I found Mae on the porch after I heard her yell, 'It's swallowing
the sky!' We stood in awe, watching the basket rise. As it lifted,

we sat in the rockers, hardly able to follow it skirt the blue while
remaining standing. Who had ever seen such a thing?

—fire shooting into cloth, the cloth expanding into
a ball, the ball ascending like a giant
building raised toward heaven.

I said, 'Mae, have you
ever?' And her silence
told me she hadn't.

We had been working
all night and sleeping
toward mid-morning

and I assumed
the whoosh was
a flock alighting,
except, instead
of moving on,
it shushed
again

and

again. It
was Mae's
hollering that
brought me outside.

Could you imagine lifting

your head from the pillow to
dream such a creature into
waking life? Can you picture

this quiet monster come to snatch you
from your nightmare of living to hoist
you gentle into the clear blue sky?

Estella Shanks, Prescott, AZ, Explains Her Profit

When they found me lying
against the wall, my legs stretched
out like a doll some child left
behind, I had tucked $326.25 in cash, a gold

watch and silver chain (real, not
nickel) in hiding
spots around
the room. Imagine

their surprise, discovering me
gone so peaceful, still and alone, all those little
drawers of coins and paper brimming. No one thinks
a mother of seven to last

seventeen years in the trade, but how
else to fill all the open mouths?
I never expected death to come

with a profit. A forty-two-year-old
whore with dependents has to keep herself
seeming young with makeup, dress

ribbons, and hair dye that poisons
over time. But the truth is
this: I wasn't supposed to live so long.

End of Times:
A letter to 'Big Billie' Betty Wagner, Silverton, CO

(found in Jan MacKell's Red Light Women of the Rocky Mountains)

Dear Billie:

No doubt you will be surprised to hear from me but I heard
you were there and I'm writing to ask how business is
and is there a chance for an old lady to come

over and go to work? There is absolutely nothing here
and I want to leave before the snow gets too deep.
If I can get a crib or go to work in

one of the joints, let me know. I wrote to Garnett and she said
there wasn't any place there I could get. Please answer
and let me know. Must close now

and put this in the mail. Bye-
bye and answer soon.
Mamie G., 200 N. 3rd St.

August 1882 Flagstaff:
A Whore's Decision

He told me to stay. He said whatever
happens, don't go south, where it drops,
he said, into a fiery hell. He meant it literal.
He said you could scream for the heat.

He said it's an oven that bakes your brain
if you breathe through your nose. If
you're too tired, he said, you'll die. I am always too
tired—men at night and then the mending and tending

bar during the day. So I can't go south for the heat,
can't go north for the mountains, taller and colder
than God, can't go west for the Mormons,
which he said to avoid at all costs. Better,

he said, to go south and get swallowed by the heat. No
whore can go back the way she came. Guess I'll stay.

The Ice Palace, Laura Evens, Leadville

Oh, when we had the ice palace! Large enough

      for any queen but made for the New Year

            at 10,000 feet. We rode the sled down

Harrison Street galloping towards the walls

      of ice like a lone mustang on

            his own stampede. You think you'd die

of the cold, but you don't. When the girls

      and I whiz by, we are no

            longer soiled. We are fresh. We are bundled,

laughing young women, fashioning a romp.

Virginia City, NV: A Timeline

1863: George Kirt robs Jessie Lester.

Later that year, while standing near the doorway, Jessie Lester sustains a bullet to the arm. Her arm is amputated. She dies from infection.

Buffalo Joe gets rowdy while drinking and is thrown onto the street where two men attack her outside the establishment. She crawls into the Sazarac Saloon, gets mouthy and is removed again. More men assault her on the street.

1864: John Collins assaults English Ida.

1865: Someone steals three thousand dollars that Rose Wilson hid about her room then pummels her to death.

Julia Shaffer (a.k.a. White) loses her jewelry to robbers.

Lizzie Hayes withstands a fractured skull via a Colt .45. (Who held it in his hands?)

Julia Bullette is beaten to death for her jewelry and money.

1867: Martha Camp hears a noise beneath her bed and peers under to see a man clasping a knife. She screams. The man escapes, leaving behind the strongbox hidden under her bed.

Martha Camp lets a man into her room for a transaction. He pulls a razor and threatens her. She screams, hollers and creates a scene. He runs off with his pants unbuttoned.

Maggie McCormick's door is riddled with bullets. The charges miss her but tear out a section of the wall. (Who pulled the triggers?)

Four men pound Ellen Farry to her death.

1877: Concerned Nevada citizens lobby to have the Senator William Stewart Law passed. This law reads:

*Any male person in the State who is more than eighteen years of age, who shall willingly and violently strike, beat, or torture the body of any maiden or woman who is more than sixteen years of age, shall be guilty of a misdemeanor, and upon conviction in any court of competent jurisdiction, shall be sentenced to be firmly tied or lashed in a standing posture to the post or pillar described in Section I of the Act.**

Saved

is a vicious
word, has teeth

and bites like a cornered
canine. *You, too,*

can be saved—
bend to hush

the dog and come
up with a punctured

thumb. Passive as a looped
leash sits the waiting.

No man insists
on the saving.

It's the wives. Not
everyone is worth

saving. When they come for
you, they are interested in

your soul. They are not interested in
your empty belly or oozing lip

or your daughter lying
listless in the back

room. No
one invests much in saving

in the temporal
world—not

really—except the rich,
and you know if they do,

they're looking for a deal.

Lil Powers on Wading in the Arkansas River, Salida, CO

I took one
step too many out
from the eddy and placed
my foot in the soft
patch of sand,
and the bottom
gave way, and
the rapid
swept me up and forward
fast as a sling-
shot. From the rocks,
Laura hollered, 'Feet
first!' so I aimed
my toes at the current
and scooted
down the river like
an oar loosed
from a canoe. I saw
the boulder coming,
bigger than a charging
bison, and I turned
my rump to kiss it
and something in
the timing
went just right,
and the rock pulled
me in side-
ways like a man
before he takes you
to bed. I got
my balance and stood
and faced the shore.
Two tentative

steps fell me
forward, ripping
my bloomers and skinning
my knees against
the pile of pebbles
that had gathered
at the boulder's base.
                    Miss Laura
hopped rocks down stream
holding up her skirts until
she stood three paces in front
of me. I wavered like
a toddler trying
out feet. But
every time I raised one leg
the other wanted to topple
and those bitty rocks were biting
my toes. Finally, I thought,
Lil, push on through, which
is what I say when I just need
to do it.
              I looked up
into the branches of the cottonwood
with its trunk wider than a judge's
bench, and fixed my eyes
on the sparkling leaves, which collected
light like the shards of a shattered mirror.
In three giant splashes, I was on the rocks,
laughing with Laura until we could barely breathe.

Death Is the Only

'Death is the only retirement from prostitution.'
—*Anonymous Prostitute, Jan McKell's* Red Light District of the Rocky
Mountains

Part I. Roll Call

Fay Anderson, Salida, Colorado, death from carbolic acid
Ettie Barker, actress, Theater Comique, Pueblo, Colorado, overdosed on
    morphine.
Blanch Garland, Bon Ton Dance Hall, Cripple Creek, Colorado, died
    from chloroform.
Nellie Rolfe also overdosed on morphine, Cripple Creek.
Cora Davis swallowed strychnine in Boulder, Colorado, New Year's
    night 1913, and died.
Stella No-last-name, also in Boulder, Colorado, dead with no cause
    listed.
May Rikand, combined alcohol and morphine in Silverton, Colorado.
Malvina López, Tombstone, committed double suicide with her
    companion, John Gibbons, by asphyxiation from burning charcoal.
Goldie Bauschell, Crystal Palace, Colorado City, jumped from second-
    story window but survived.
Effie Pryor and Allie Ellis of Boulder, Colorado attempted double
    suicide by morphine. Allie survived.
Nora McCord, Salida, Colorado summoned death through unidentified
    pills. Nora, too, was unidentified. She never used her real name.

*Part II. Madam Maddie Silk Narrates, Boulder, CO, New Year's Night
1913*

When we nudged the door a little, it gave.
Cora lay curled on her bed like she was in a womb,
naked, except for the silk stockings which she prized.

It took a moment, and Officer Parkhill saw a breath
from her chest, and then we all held our own: she was
alive. Officer Parkhill and the other policeman

lifted her off the bed and carried her down
the stairs, Mr. Parkhill lifting her shoulders
and leaning her head against

his chest. This is when Cora revived long
enough to empty the contents of her abdomen.
She turned her head and heaved onto Officer

Parkhill's chest all the poison in the world.
The officers transported Cora by car,
and I rode in back. The 20-degrees

surrounding us wanted its silence,
and we gave it. I had wrapped Cora
in a big bear blanket, but she settled

back into the deepness of dying. Here,
we delivered her to the county
hospital. *I'll stay*. I said. *Mr. Parkhill,
your suit is ruined*. He agreed.

The men took their hats and their way,
and I settled into a night of quiet. 1913,
unlucky at best. Cora died the next day.

Pearl de Vere, Cripple Creek, CO

The storm arrived just after four,
vomit-green sky carrying thunder
heads full of hail which were hurled

in a fury.
          Only Mabel had company. I sat
in my window seat and watched two crows

shaken from the evergreen, the wind bending
the tree like it was going
to swoon. White draped every curve of the ground

like it was covering a bride. Then, the lightning—
the kind that shudders the earth
instead of strikes—arrived with grumbling

thunder. Those dirty
clouds were washed clean
in the downpour. When it subsided

like a man just emptied, the fog appeared
like a slow old burro. Stubborn, too, it
stayed, burying us in the clouds.

We arrived

                    in the dark—
a middle-of-the-night
affair—the stagecoach's

splinters biting
my bits, and grease hugging
my hem and blending with my boot

and nail heads providing strips
of cloth from the creases in my dress.
The driver dropped

my case down onto the road,
splashing me muddier. So
imagine my surprise when

my weariness found a bed and the sun
rose and so did I, opening
the shutters to see three

women on ponies riding by
with no man as escort. The sun
was already warming up

the blue, and they rode single file
out a little distance in
the brush, riding astride, not

side-saddle, but I could tell
they were women and heading
somewhere on their own

mounts. This was the moment
before anyone knew who
or what I was or did or why

I came, before anyone knew I was
as filthy on the inside as my dress
hanging off that peg. Just three

ponies in the distance pointed
north, the sunlight filtering the eastern
air and me, glancing out the window.

Big Nose Kate Mentions Ulises

Before Doc ever arrived, Ulises led me into the darkness
of his room—his, instead of mine—and bent me over the foot
of the bed. He closed the door and then black descended

like the bottom of a coal mine. He might've sliced
my throat. But he didn't. I whispered, *Don't finish inside.*
But he did. Words exchanged between us like foreign

coins handled in the wrong country. When he was done,
he said, *gracias*, and I said *köszönöm.* He didn't pay, and I
didn't ask him to. I'd simply wanted him, so I didn't mind.

Silver Heels

*'So many yarns have been spun about the story of Silver
Heels that the truth seems lost to history ... In Colorado,
only Mt. Silver Heels, located north of Fairplay, as well
as a namesake creek and even a mine with its short-lived
camp, attest to her ever existing at all.'*

—*Jan McKell,* Brothels, Bordellos, and Bad Girls

A mountain ain't a bad thing
to have named in your memory; it's bigger
than a tombstone and is like to last longer.

It ain't never going to move. And if it comes
with a creek, why then that's a bonus, like a bit
of lace on a bonnet. Like a bow on a girl's

dress, there ain't one narrative about me
that's straight. The truth so wavers
that I can't track it anymore.

Was I an 'angel of mercy?' Hell, no.
Do not romanticize my kind. I cared
no less than any Christian. If a nun

tended to those miners, what would she
be called? If you judge my behavior two
separate ways—tending to living men

and tending to men who are dying—
then you're inciting a divide
where there is none. Tending

is tending. Let me tell you a secret:
No woman on earth is an angel. Not
one. An angel is an angel, and they're hard

to come by. Ain't
no angel had a mountain named
for her, neither. Least not in these parts.

I'll take my mountain, my stream, and my mine,
and I'll let you all keep spinning the tales, trying
so hard to fathom what simply ain't hard

to fathom. One miner, so in love with me,
painted my portrait on a saloon floor. Six
floorboards across form my blonde hair,

fixed pretty, with boots stomping on my smile
every time some mouth wanted whisky. All
these ways to remember. My dancing silver

boots. More stories than leaves on an aspen.
I got me a mountain, which means even
in the freezing months, under a bright

full moon, while everyone else has vanished—
the bartender, the schoolmarm, the sheriff and those
scruffy miners—while everyone else forgets them all,

I'm always going to shine.

Notes

Maxine, Tombstone, Arizona
Quote taken from Jan McKell's book *Red Light Women of the Rocky Mountains*, p. 26.
Virginia City, NV: A Timeline
Found in Michael Rutter's *Upstairs Girls: Prostitution in the American West*

Acknowledgements

This book took years of research, traveling, and writing to create. Special thanks to my mom, Elaine K. Williams, who was there at the beginning of the project, in Bisbee, Arizona, encouraging me and helping me explore. Also thanks to my sister, Allyson Williams-Yee, for creating the artwork for the cover on short and loving notice. I am grateful for Penelope Layland, the book's editor, whose thoughts and attention to details via conversation and careful reading helped the book emerge more fully. The support of Paul Hetherington and Jen Webb has been both inspirational and instrumental to my writing and living in Australia. And, finally, thanks to Shane Strange, for his support, guidance, and bottomless pail of patience in the production and publication of this book. Without the help of all of these beautiful humans, this book never would have come into being.

'I Am Legend,' 'Lydia Taylor,' 'Soiled Dove,' 'Sometimes a Woman,' 'Maxine, Tombstone, AZ,' and 'Some Nights' published in *Axon*, Issue 9.1, 2019.
'Roll Call of the Fancy Ladies, Yavapai Country'; 'Death Is Only'; 'End of Times,' published in *Peregrinos y sus letras,* September 2018.

About the Author

Kimberly K. Williams has an MFA in Creative Writing from the University of Texas El Paso. Kimberly was short-listed for the University of Canberra's Vice-Chancellor's Poetry Prize in 2019, and her poems appear in many journals and anthologies around the world. After twenty years of writing and teaching in the U.S. Southwest, Kimberly moved to Canberra to work on a PhD. She is originally from Detroit, Michigan.

Printed in Australia
Ingram Content Group Australia Pty Ltd
AUHW020939051223
387493AU00002B/13

9 780645 009064